LOOKING INSIDE

SUNKEN TREASURE

Ron Schultz

ILLUSTRATED BY

Nick Gadbois and Peter Aschwanden

John Muir Publications

Santa Fe, New Mexico

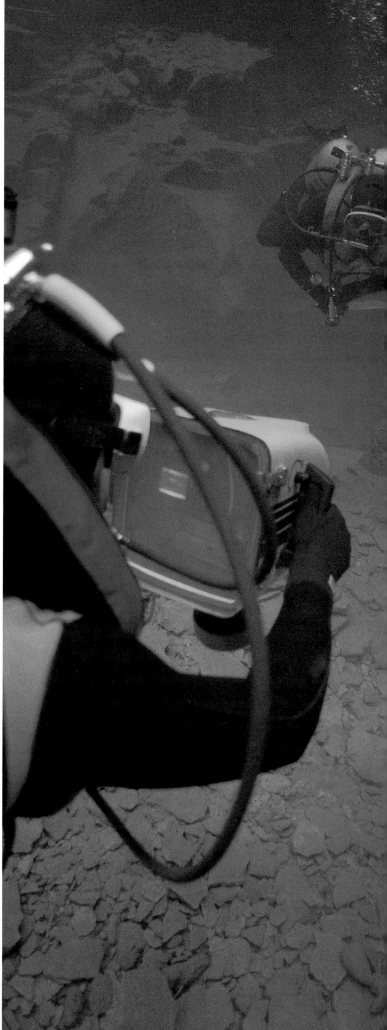

ACKNOWLEDGMENTS

This book would not have been possible without the open doors, willing cooperation, and uncompromised dedication of the National Park Service's Submerged Cultural Resource Unit: Dan Lenihan, Larry Murphy, Fran Day, and John Brooks. I would also like to thank the staff of John Muir Publications for continuing to unlock the treasures of knowledge.

This book is dedicated to Laura Del Mar
An extraordinary educator

John Muir Publications, P.O. Box 613, Santa Fe, NM 87504

First edition. First printing December 1992

Library of Congress Cataloging-in-Publication Data
Schultz, Ron (Ronald), 1951-
    Looking inside sunken treasure / Ron Schultz ;
  illustrated by Peter Aschwanden and Nick Gadbois.
  —1st ed.
      p.   cm. — (X-ray vision)
    Includes index.
    ISBN 1-56261-074-0
    1. Underwater archaeology. 2. Underwater
  archaeology — United States. 3. Shipwrecks —
  United States. 4. Treasure-trove — United States.
  5. United States — Antiquities.   I. Aschwanden,
  Peter. II. Gadbois, Nick. III. Title. IV. Series.
  CC77.U5S34   1993
  930.1'028'04—dc20   92-30991
                                            CIP

Design: Ken Wilson
Illustrations: Peter Aschwanden and Nick Gadbois
Typeface: ITC Benguiat
Printer: Inland Press
Cover photo: National Park Service

Distributed to the book trade by
W. W. Norton & Co.
500 Fifth Avenue
New York, NY 10110

Distributed to the education market by
The Wright Group
19201 120th Avenue NE
Bothell, WA 98011

National Park Service

CONTENTS

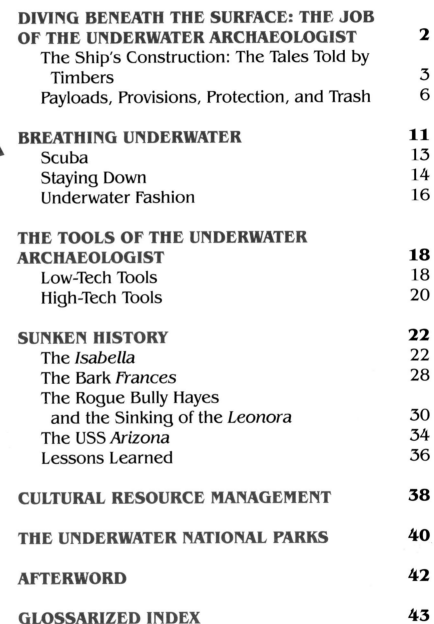

INTRODUCTION   **1**

DIVING BENEATH THE SURFACE: THE JOB OF THE UNDERWATER ARCHAEOLOGIST   **2**
The Ship's Construction: The Tales Told by Timbers   3
Payloads, Provisions, Protection, and Trash   6

BREATHING UNDERWATER   **11**
Scuba   13
Staying Down   14
Underwater Fashion   16

THE TOOLS OF THE UNDERWATER ARCHAEOLOGIST   **18**
Low-Tech Tools   18
High-Tech Tools   20

SUNKEN HISTORY   **22**
The *Isabella*   22
The Bark *Frances*   28
The Rogue Bully Hayes
  and the Sinking of the *Leonora*   30
The USS *Arizona*   34
Lessons Learned   36

CULTURAL RESOURCE MANAGEMENT   **38**

THE UNDERWATER NATIONAL PARKS   **40**

AFTERWORD   **42**

GLOSSARIZED INDEX   **43**

*T*he great winds had already cracked the main mast in two. Waves of seawater poured in from all sides of the wooden sailing ship. Sailors scurried to tie down whatever could be secured, but it was a losing battle. The rough and untamed sea would claim the booty of yet another galleon. Swiftly, the mighty ship sank beneath the waves, as all hands clung desperately to tiny life rafts, buffeted like splinters by the raging storm. All was lost; cargo, possessions, weaponry, and stores, gobbled by the sea, destined to lie in the briny deep for ages to come.

INTRODUCTION

Hundreds of years later, a shipwreck can reveal to scientists details about the lives and times of the people who fell to the depths of the oceans with the ships they sailed. These scientists are underwater archaeologists. "Archaeology" comes from two Greek words, *archaios*, meaning "ancient things," and *logos*, "all about." Underwater archaeology, then, is learning all about ancient things found in the water. As we will also see, the things found in the water might come from ships that went down in more recent times, too.

Shipwrecks aren't the only things underwater archaeologists study. There are many ancient coastal civilizations that have slipped beneath the tides. But the majority of an underwater archaeologist's work, the work we will observe here, involves exploring the remains of sunken ships. These watery relics are time capsules of the moment they were swallowed up by the water. When unsealed by an underwater archaeologist, these treasure chests hold secrets about how people of the time treated each other, about people traveling to new lands, and about how they behaved when life became very dangerous. They speak about high adventures—about encounters with pirates—as well as about daily, humdrum chores. But most of all, they capture our imaginations with a history of a time we can only know through the yarns and legends contained in their now shivered timbers.

Let us don our underwater gear and dive down to explore the graves of great ships. These underwater archaeological museums are not for spoiling and looting but for looking back to a time when life was very different. So, into the water me hearties, and let us see the booty still being held in Neptune's domain.

National Park Service photo by Dan Lenihan

DIVING BENEATH THE SURFACE

THE JOB OF THE UNDERWATER ARCHAEOLOGIST

The underwater archaeologist's job is not just recovering or locating artifacts from the distant and recent past; it is also mapping the exposed remains of the sunken ship and studying the shipwreck site itself, how the shipwreck has been scattered across the water's bottom. The sites are carefully mapped with cameras, drawings, and even video cameras.

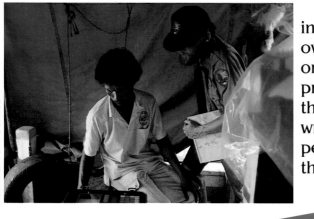

National Park Service

Underwater archaeologists also spend time working out of the water, too. Like detectives, they pore over written history files, and they try to uncover the original drawings of the sunken ships, which might provide some clues for patching together the story they see unfolding underwater. They also dig up written sources that give them a sense of the way people in that period of time acted. By combining all this information with their actual underwater site observations, archaeologists can re-create what life on board that ship might have been like before it drifted down to its watery grave.

When an underwater archaeologist dives down to a wreck, there are five basic areas that he or she explores: (1) the way the ship was built; (2) the cargo it was carrying on board; (3) the ship's stores, or supplies for the voyage; (4) the ship's weapons and the way the ship was trimmed, its riggings (the kinds of sails, sail lines, and anchors), lighting fixtures, steering wheels, mastheads, and

Photo by John D. Brooks

THE CUMBERLAND 1871

mechanical operations; and (5) the ship's bilge, where the ballast, heavy substances like iron or stones stored at the very bottom of the ship to steady it, was kept. In addition, being at the very bottom, the bilge was typically the ship's giant trash can, filled with waste from all quarters.

THE SHIP'S CONSTRUCTION: THE TALES TOLD BY TIMBERS

The design of these water travelers and the way they were built are often dead giveaways to the kind of work they performed. Some of the large Spanish galleons were basically large, slow sea trucks They were designed with deep hulls to carry lots of goods and didn't require a large crew. So, an underwater archaeologist would expect to find small crew quarters. He or she would also be looking for a deep hull, or body of the ship, because these vessels traveled far across the deep ocean, and a deep hull provided more cargo space and a more stable trip. Of course, the slow pace of these lumbering ships made them ripe for pirating, a fate that sent many to the bottom.

Galleon

Clipper

During the California gold rush, majestic, streamlined wind runners called clippers sped along the seas. The construction of the clippers' hulls allowed them to literally cut through the water. These great tall ships required large crews to hoist all the sails that allowed them to race with the wind. So, in exploring a ship-wrecked clipper, an archaeologist would expect to find a large living space for sailors. One of the things an archaeologist might try to find out is how the crew was treated and how their comfort and safety was considered, or not. He or she could discover this by measuring the size of the crew's quarters and comparing it to the size of the officers' quarters.

The construction of a ship also reveals the kinds of water a boat traveled through. A deep-hulled oceanfaring vessel would look completely different from a riverboat, whose shallow bottom would quickly separate it from a Great Lakes freighter.

Other clues the underwater archaeologist looks for are the materials used to build the ship—where the wood might have come from, how it was assembled, how the metals were forged. This information allows the archaeologist to determine the year the vessel was built, and it can also say something about the superstitions of those sailing within them. For example, there was a time when sailors wouldn't sail on boats with metal hulls, because they knew that wood floats and metal sinks. So, the shift

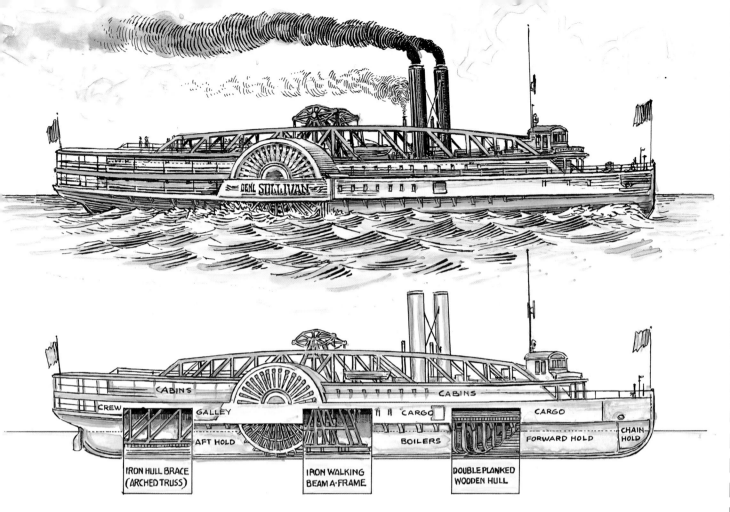

CABINS   CABINS
CREW   GALLEY   CARGO   CARGO
          AFT HOLD   BOILERS   FORWARD HOLD   CHAIN HOLD

IRON HULL BRACE   IRON WALKING   DOUBLE PLANKED
(ARCHED TRUSS)   BEAM A-FRAME   WOODEN HULL

to boats built with metal hulls had to first combine metal and wood or the sailors wouldn't trust that they were seaworthy.

One of the biggest changes in ship construction took place when steam power replaced wind power. This innovation completely changed the shape and size of ships. It meant bigger and often faster ships, but like the Titanic, they sank just as easily as the wind-driven crafts.

Steamship

PAYLOADS, PROVISIONS, PROTECTION, AND TRASH

The Cargo

Located deep in the hold of a ship is its cargo—the precious payload—which is packed tightly and carefully, with no room for useless extras. From the cargo, we can learn something about the people who sent the ship off toward its distant destinations. We can find out, for example, what they thought was valuable for those on the other side of the sea. The cargo might have included all kinds of special equipment and life-sustaining supplies for new colonies of settlers in the New World. Or it might have contained gold and silver leaving the New World for the coffers of European royalty. Or, more recently, it might have contained furniture heading for market.

Photo by Emory Kristof, courtesy of National Geographic Society

The cargo can also reveal the villainous traits of those who sailed a ship. In many cases, the manifest of a ship, the list itemizing its cargo, doesn't contain everything found in the hold. The history of the sea is filled with rogues and rascals. And an archaeologist may discover booty that was being smuggled on the ship before it met its unhappy fate. Smuggling on the high seas was a common practice, and shipwrecks can divulge wicked tales about the culture of such times.

The Ship's Stores

The ship's stores contained all those things necessary for the survival of the sailors on board. From the foodstuffs to the medical supplies for healing the sick or injured, the material in the ship's stores exposes the actual knowledge a society had at the time about surviving a long journey. This is where the science of the

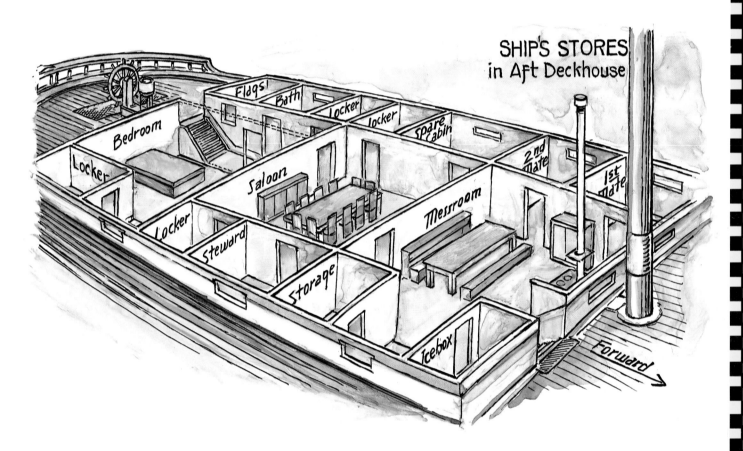

SHIP'S STORES in Aft Deckhouse

present observes the science of the past. For example, within the water-soaked food casks, scientists can detect the only surviving remains of how these societies tried to preserve their food.

In addition, because a ship has such limited space, almost everything on board had to be absolutely necessary for the trip. Of course, the sailors were experts at stowing their own personal prizes in their own tiny space. When discovered by an underwater archaeologist, these small but essential reminders of home, like pictures or good luck charms or a carved ivory box, speak volumes about who these people were.

Archaeologists studing a half-buried cannon

Weapons and Trim

Venturing out onto the high seas was always a dangerous and risky business. You never knew when you might come across a ship flying the Jolly Roger barreling straight for your broadside. Battle frigates weren't the only ships that carried weapons. Cannons and swivel guns were kept on almost all vessels. But not all ships had their cannons ready to fire through their bulwarks, the raised sides of the ship.

Where a captain kept his weapons can tell archaeologists what perils he thought he might encounter on his journey. If his cannons were being stored as ballast, adding weight in the bilge to steady the ship, that indicates he wasn't fearing the likes of Bluebeard to come swooping down on him. If they were on deck raring to blast a mighty hole in the port side of an adversary, the ship's priorities were obviously different.

These weapons of defense and destruction also help date the ship, provide clues about what kind of ship it was, and even reveal from where it might have sailed. Underwater archaeologists have also established what really happened during historical events by examining ammunition found on board a sunken ship. In the case of the Spanish Armada ship, the *Santa Maria de la Rosa*, archaeologists discovered that faulty shot on board probably made it impossible to stop the attack of the English. Was it bad ammo that sunk the famed Spanish Armada, not the superior battle plan of the English?

Underwater archaeologists also look at a ship's rigging, lanterns, steering mechanisms, hearths, and decorative designs to paint a picture of the time in which it sailed. For example, even after hundreds of years beneath the water, the hearths, or cook boxes, on these ships can be tested by scientists with a technique that reveals the date it was last used. Broken or twisted anchor lines could hold the answer to how the ship might have foundered beneath the fury of a devastating storm or why it ran aground on a reef. Its fancy decorations can provide clues to its dating and the culture that sent it to sea.

Photo by Emory Kristof, courtesy of National Geographic Society

The Bilge

In the darkest, dankest, and dreariest depths of a ship lies the bilge. Being at the very bottom of things, the bilge is often the final resting place for all the rotten waste of a ship's voyage. It is also the storage area for the ship's ballast, which helps archaeologists determine the origin of the ship and what stopovers it might have made. Finding stones from Africa in a wreck at the bottom of the South Seas means the ship probably spent some time on the dark continent.

It is within the rotted waste disposal of the bilge that underwater archaeologists find some of their greatest treasures. Archaeologists, whether on land or at sea, have traditionally discovered remarkable things about the cultures they are examining from their waste piles, called midden. For example, finding the remains of rat bones that have been butchered and gnawed indicates the crew was under enough stress from a lack of food to resort to eating rats. The bilge, though often of little monetary value, is typically a high priority for underwater archaeologists. ❧

BREATHING UNDERWATER

Early deep-sea divers looked something like mini-submarines. They wore very large and cumbersome, completely enclosed, heavy helmeted diving gear. They are called dry suits, because the diver stayed dry inside them. (Actually, this gear is similar in many ways to what astronauts used to wear for space launches.) Once the aquanauts were in the water, air was pumped down to them through a long hose from a ship above.

Skin diving, so called because for the most part no protective suit is worn, was another early approach to exploring the underwater world. A diver used only a snorkel, mask, and fins to get about. The mask strapped snugly around the head and had a glass lens that covered the eyes and nose. Today, a mask is standard equipment for all underwater diving.

A snorkel is another standard piece of diving equipment. Its name comes from the Dutch word, *schnorchel*, which described a breathing tube devised for submarines in the 1930s. For divers, a snorkel is basically a rubber tube with a mouthpiece at one end. It is used on the surface of the water, so a diver can continue to breathe normally while partially submerged.

Since people weren't born with webbed feet to propel us through the water, we had to invent fins. This is also a standard piece of equipment for all underwater diving. Fins free our hands to pick things up, use cameras, make notes, and clear away debris.

Fins Snorkel & Mask

A LITTLE WATER SCIENCE

How does a diver move in the water while wearing so much heavy gear?

On land, air molecules are far apart. Unlike water molecules, which are packed tightly together, air molecules are far apart and can be easily squished into smaller spaces or compressed, like the compressed air in a diving tank. Because of this squishability, air doesn't support the weight we are carrying, it is just pushed away.

Water, however, is 800 times denser than air. That means if you were to put water into a one-inch-high column and air into another one-inch-high column, there would be 800 times more water molecules in the column than air molecules. Water molecules don't compress, so water supports the weight of objects and makes them feel lighter. They actually weigh the same; the weight is just supported. The next time you are in a pool, try to pick up a parent or a larger friend. You'll be surprised at how much more weight you can lift in the water.

The main restriction for skin divers is that they have to stay fairly close to the surface or dive down only as deep as they can hold their breath. Prior to the invention of masks and snorkels, holding your breath and diving like the clam divers of the Orient was the only alternative. None of these techniques are especially suited for underwater archaeology.

AUTHOR

SCUBA

Fortunately for underwater archaeologists, Jacques Cousteau and Emil Gagnan invented the self-contained underwater breathing apparatus commonly called "scuba."

Scuba gear makes us more fishlike, or at least allows us to breathe underwater without being tied to an air line from above. In addition to a mask, fins, and a snorkel, scuba divers wear a steel or aluminum tank filled with pressurized compressed air. The air is compressed so that more air can fit into the tank. Valves are fitted on top of the tanks so that a regulator can be attached. The regulator allows the compressed air to be released at just the right pressure for the depth to which the diver is descending.

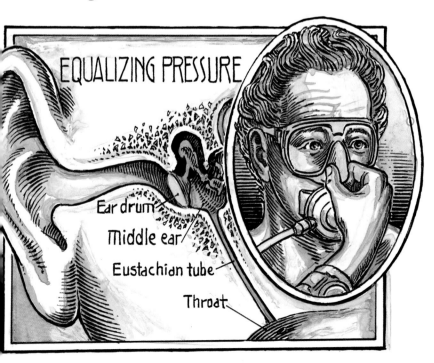

EQUALIZING PRESSURE

Ear drum
Middle ear
Eustachian tube
Throat

KEEPING THE EARS CLEAR

You may not realize it, but the body has lots of different places where it holds air. We usually think air is kept just in the lungs, but there are also areas in the sinuses and the middle ear where air collects. As a diver descends into the water, the water pressure increases. Since the air being breathed is equal to the pressure surrounding it (remember the regulator?), the lungs are, for the most part, unaffected. Actually, this is true for all the body spaces but the ears.

The middle ear is connected to the throat by a tiny tube called the Eustachian tube. The air that travels up that tube helps to equalize the pressure coming from outside the ear. By opening the tube and allowing air in, we can change the pressure in the middle ear. This is done by yawning, swallowing, or pushing out the lower jaw. But as a diver descends underwater, the pressure increases so much that the Eustachian tube needs to be continually opened up. If it isn't kept open and the pressure balanced, the increased water pressure will keep it from opening at all. When this happens, the air pressure on the middle ear is increased, and it can cause painful and dangerous injuries to the diver's ear. By opening the tube every few feet as he descends, a diver can equalize the pressure outside and inside the ear.

Water pressure increases as a diver goes deeper, because there is more water on top pressing down. If you've ever dived down to the bottom of a pool, you've probably felt the effects of water pressure on your ears as you went deeper.

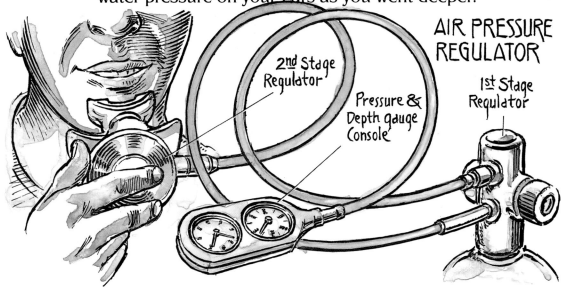

AIR PRESSURE REGULATOR

2nd Stage Regulator

Pressure & Depth gauge Console

1st Stage Regulator

Air pressure regulators have to deliver air to the diver no matter how great the water pressure. To accommodate this, there are two parts to a regulator: one attached to the tank valve, and one with the mouthpiece and gauge that automatically reduces the pressure of the compressed air so it can be breathed. They are connected by a pressure hose, which also has a gauge on it that shows the diver how much air is left in the tank.

STAYING DOWN

Of course, a diver must be able to stay underwater without bobbing up to the surface. Basically, there are three ways of being in the water: you can float, sink, or be neutral or stationary underwater (not sinking or floating but still submerged). At different times, a scuba diver has to do all three. The diver wants to be able to sink to the bottom. When he's on the bottom, he wants to be neutral, or remain suspended in the water without having to fight against sinking or floating. Then, when he's coming up to the surface, the diver wants to be able to float slowly upward.

divers decompressing in shallow water

THE EFFECTS OF NITROGEN

The deeper a diver goes, the greater the level of nitrogen in the body. This occurs because the added water pressure doesn't allow the nitrogen to be released as it would be on land. This becomes a very serious problem for divers who are at a depth of more than 100 feet for a long period of time. It can cause hallucinations, and a diver can lose his or her sense of direction. Fortunately, these conditions disappear as soon as a diver leaves great depths.

In addition to the problems of becoming disoriented, nitrogen absorption can adversely affect divers if they return to the surface too quickly. If a diver rises slowly, the body will naturally get rid of the nitrogen that has been absorbed. If the ascent is too fast, the nitrogen can't be eliminated and can form bubbles inside the body. This effect, called either decompression sickness or the "bends," can result in serious injuries, even paralysis.

The bends can be avoided. By using decompression tables, a diver can figure out how long he can stay at certain depths to avoid the bends. If he remains in deeper water longer than his body can quickly eliminate the nitrogen, he must stay underwater at shallow depths to allow the nitrogen to be released. This is called decompression. In some cases, a 25-minute dive to depths over 150 feet might require a diver to decompress in shallow water for up to a couple of hours. A five-minute dive to those depths might not require any decompression.

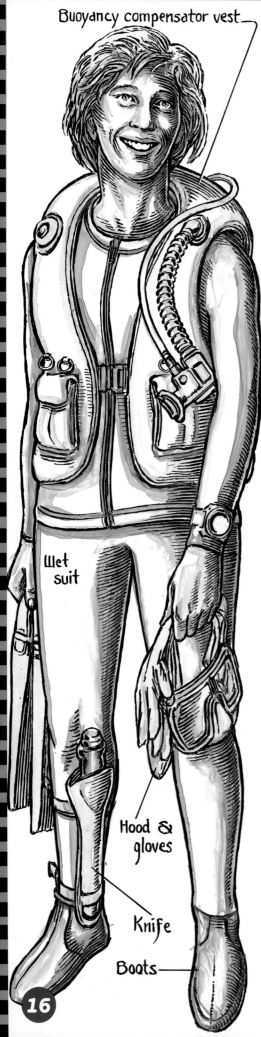

Buoyancy compensator vest

Wet suit

Hood & gloves

Knife

Boots

Special diving equipment was developed to accomplish this balancing act. Going down is fairly easy. Lead weights attached to a belt allow a diver to sink down. You might think that because humans are heavy, we'd automatically sink. But because we've got air in our lungs, we are basically buoyant, that is, we tend to float. The more buoyant a diver is, the more weight he will have to wear to get to the bottom.

As a diver goes deeper in the water and the water pressure increases, buoyancy tends to decrease. This is due to the weight of the water on top of the diver. That's why divers also wear buoyancy compensators. These devices can be filled with a little air as a diver descends to increase buoyancy so that the diver can remain suspended at any depth in the water. When it is time to go back up, the buoyancy compensator can be inflated fully to aid the slow climb to the surface.

UNDERWATER FASHION

Because water absorbs heat from the body, divers need to wear special underwater clothing. For most diving conditions, divers use wet suits. They trap a small amount of water inside them which is quickly heated by the body. The insulation of the suit prevents the heat from escaping. To make sure that too much water doesn't creep in, a wet suit needs to be a snug fit.

Dry suits are for colder water. They keep a diver warmer because they are insulated with air rather than water. But because they have air in them, they make a diver more buoyant and are harder to control.

To protect divers from slicing and dicing their water-softened hands on coral reefs or on pieces of jagged metal jutting from shipwrecks, most divers wear special gloves. Also, because most of the body's heat escapes through the head and feet, they wear hoods and socklike boots.

A diver may also need a few gauges and tools. Depth gauges are important, because divers have to be careful about how deep they go and how long they stay in very deep water. They also need to know how long they've been under water, so a diving watch is required. An underwater compass is also valuable, especially when diving in areas where the visibility in the water is low.

One of the most important tools a diver carries is a diving knife. This isn't for fighting off creatures from the deep but for cutting cord or netting, sticking underneath rocks or shells, and prying, digging, or pounding. A diving knife is normally strapped to the inside of the diver's ankle or the forearm so it can be easily reached. The last thing a diver wants is to be trapped in an abandoned fishing net 75 feet beneath the surface and unable to reach his knife. ❧

ivers consulting underwater map at Fort Jefferson National Monument

THE TOOLS OF THE ARCHAEOLOGIST

Things can get pretty murky and treacherous underwater. The currents at some shipwreck sites are so dangerous that it would make even a tough old scalawag like Bluebeard turn gray. But there are times when underwater archaeologists must ride out these wild currents to secure the data they need. Since fighting currents can be exhausting, underwater archaeologists can't make frequent trips back and forth to bring down all the tools they may need to measure and document the wrecks. They also can't use bulky or awkward devices. The key: the simpler the tools, the better.

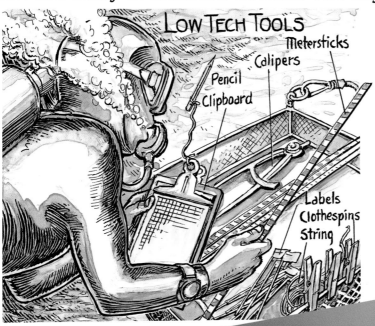

LOW-TECH TOOLS

In this era of high technology, super-sophisticated electronics, space age retractable laser beams, and ultra speedy computers, the primary tools of an underwater archaeologist are surprisingly low tech: string, measuring tapes, clothespins, and a protractor for drawing angles.

The first step in understanding a shipwreck is to map it. Once on the

National Park Service photo by Dan Lenihan

wreck site, a straight line is drawn to measure the length of the ill-fated wreckage. Then any curves or angles of the soggy ship remains are marked out. Slowly, line by line, as if drawing ribs on a watery spinal cord, the skeleton of the wreck is resurrected around the first straight line. It's a process that takes lots and lots of measurements—while fighting currents, cold water, nitrogen absorption, and poor visibility.

Photo by John D. Brooks

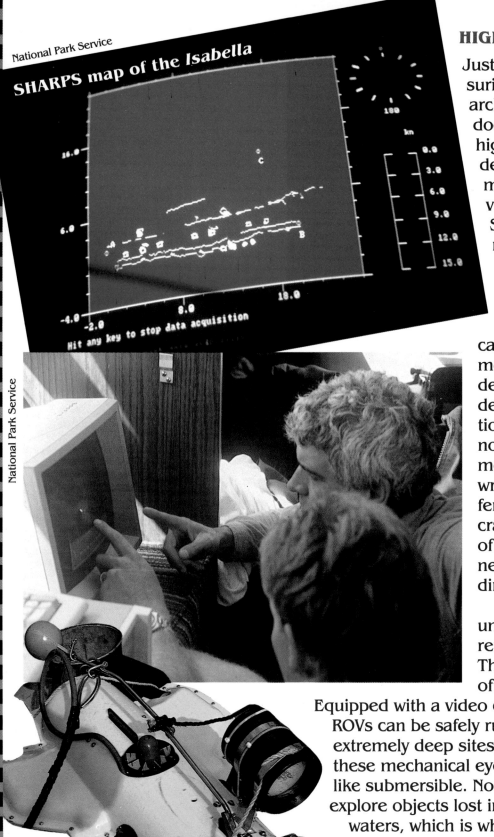

SHARPS map of the Isabella

180

kn

0.0

3.0

6.0

9.0

12.0

15.0

16.0

6.0

-4.0

-2.0

8.0

10.0

Hit any key to stop data acquisition

**Remote
Operated
Vehicle
(ROV)**

National Park Service photo by Ann Belleman

HIGH-TECH TOOLS

Just because the preferred measuring tools of an underwater archaeologist are low tech doesn't mean that there aren't higher technologies being developed. One computerized mapping tool that has been very effective is called the SHARPS (sonic highly accurate range position system).

In this technique, divers set three electronic devices into three different areas of the site. One of the divers carries an electronic computer mouse. Pressing the mouse delivers a signal to the other devices. From their fixed positions, they can establish and note the exact position of the mouse. A diver encircles the wreck site and punches in different positions around the craft, creating a dotted outline of the area. The computer connects the dots to create a three-dimensional map of the site.

Another high-tech tool of the underwater archaeologist is the remote operated vehicle (ROV). These robots of the deep are often called swimming eyes. Equipped with a video camera, the joystick-operated ROVs can be safely run from the surface. At extremely deep sites, a person can operate one of these mechanical eyes from a small diving bell-like submersible. Normally, ROVs are used to explore objects lost in extremely deep or frigid waters, which is where divers will have the most difficulties.

A recent underwater technology, still in development, uses laser beams to map sunken treasure. To use this laser imaging process, divers pull a large scanning device back and forth across the wreck to be mapped. The images are then processed by a computer, revealing a very distinct image of the wreck and its final resting ground.

Ah, the adventure of the open water: the thrill of the water's spray across the ship's bow, the gentle rocking of the waves, the exuberance of a dancing dolphin escort. But with the adventures sometimes comes terror—of a lashing storm snapping the mainsail mast, flooding the ship, flinging it like an empty matchbox, and splintering it against the rocky shore.

Let us excavate some of the stories of ships who met a ghastly fate after encountering the ocean's fury. The National Park Service's Submerged Cultural Resource Unit (SCRU) is America's leading underwater archaeology group. It is dedicated to preserving and protecting the shipwrecks along our waterways and throughout our territories. The SCRU will help us do our detective work.

So, come along, and let us dive down into the watery deep. There are ships to be explored and wondrous treasures from the past to be found.

ISABELLA

THE *ISABELLA*

Under the command of Captain William Ryan, the *Isabella*, with her puffy "apple-cheeked" front section, bid farewell to her British Isle home on October 30, 1829, and set sail for America. This square-sailed, twin-masted brig rounded Cape Horn in the spring of 1830 and headed north toward the Pacific Northwest. Laden with guns, ammunition, beads, cooking pots, candles, mirrors, combs, buttons, and shoes as well as medicine, tobacco, and tea, she was the annual supply ship for the Hudson's Bay Company's Pacific Northwest fur trade operation.

It was earlier in 1829 that the Hudson's Bay Company had received word that their supply ship, the *William & Ann*, had been lost with all hands aboard. The *William & Ann* was the first victim of the mighty and treacherous Columbia River.

Needing to get supplies to its outposts, the *Isabella* was dispatched to replace the *William & Ann*. On May 2, 1830, the ship entered the mouth of the Columbia River. The currents were strong, and the winds were high. It was then that Captain Ryan made his disastrous mistake. Having never been on the Columbia, he mistook an important landmark and ran the

Isabella onto a sandbar, later to be known as Sand Island. With the surf pounding the *Isabella*'s sides, Captain Ryan gave the order to begin dumping cargo overboard to try and save her. But the rough surf threw her back aground, and she lost her rudder. By evening the ship was abandoned, and the crew rowed up the Columbia to the Hudson's Bay Company's Fort Vancouver outpost to tell their sorry tale.

The crew returned to the wreck and cut a hole in the side of the ship to drain some of the water. Over the next few weeks, they were able to salvage about 75 percent of the *Isabella*'s cargo. On June 2, 1830, the *Isabella*, now lying on her side, finally split apart and disappeared beneath the surface. She wouldn't be heard from again for 156 years.

In 1986, a commercial fisherman snagged his nets on something large. He reported the incident to the Columbia River Maritime Museum, and divers went down and discovered the wreck. About a year later, archaeologists from the SCRU were called in to begin their research.

After the SCRU looked through all the available historical information, the archaeologists believed they had found the remains of the *Isabella*. It was now up to them to determine if what was *thought* was in fact true. They made a list of all the physical evidence they might expect to find if this was the *Isabella*. First, they

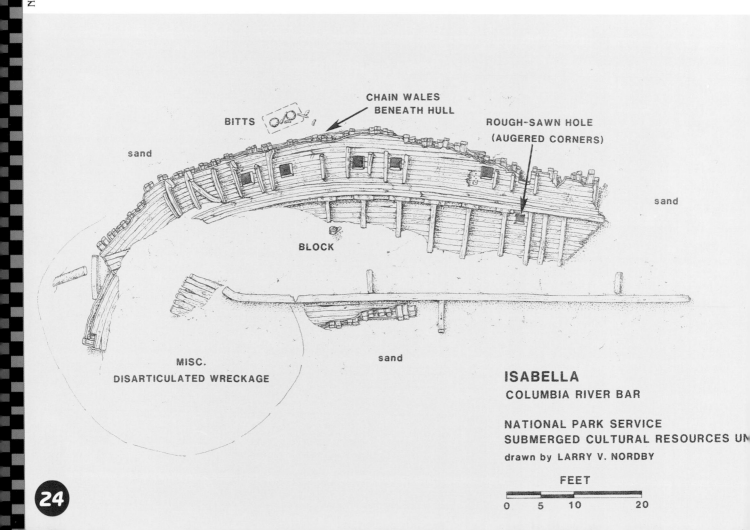

CHAIN WALES
BENEATH HULL

BITTS

ROUGH-SAWN HOLE
(AUGERED CORNERS)

sand

sand

BLOCK

MISC.
DISARTICULATED WRECKAGE

sand

ISABELLA
COLUMBIA RIVER BAR

NATIONAL PARK SERVICE
SUBMERGED CULTURAL RESOURCES UN

drawn by LARRY V. NORDBY

FEET

0   5   10   20

Top and bottom: National Park Service

needed to verify the ship's construction. Was it an "apple-cheeked" vessel, that is, did it have a rounded, apple-shaped front? Was the wood English oak that was naturally bent rather than sawed? Was it double framed? Did the ship look like a merchant ship rather than a warship? Was she larger than 90 feet in length or have a hold deeper than 17 feet? Was she twin-masted? The archaeologists also made a list of the kinds of material artifacts they thought they might find in the ship's cargo, stores, and bilge. They also wanted to make sure it was indeed near Sand Island and that the ship's rudder was missing. In addition, if it was the *Isabella*, there should be evidence of a hole cut in her side.

When they arrived at the site between Oregon and Washington State, the weather was cold. So was the water. They already knew the site would be very dangerous. The Columbia bar, where the Columbia River meets the Pacific Ocean, is the most dangerous area for navigation in the United States. Even at slack tides, those calmer tides between high and

Diver fighting strong currents of the Columbia River

25

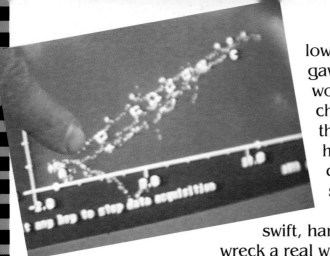

SHARPS computer image of the *Isabella*

low tides, the currents are rough. These tides only gave the divers about three hours a day to do their work. Even then it was treacherous. When the tides changed directions, they did so incredibly swiftly. By the time the divers got back to the boat, they barely had the strength to pull themselves on board. These dangerous conditions were made worse by the strong currents that continually slammed the divers into the diving platform. They reported that the swift, hammering currents made the 40-foot dive to the wreck a real white-knuckler.

Besides all this, visibility in the water was poor, and the wreck was covered with fishnets. The divers often became entangled in the snagged nets and had to hack their way out with their knives. Because of the 40-degree waters, they had to wear cumbersome dry suits, rather than the easier-to-maneuver-in wet suits, to do their work.

Despite these difficulties, archaeologists determined the vessel was indeed the *Isabella*. It did lie close to Sand Island, at the recorded spot it was lost. It was a beamy vessel, as these brigs were, with an apple-cheeked, puffed-out bow, and the remains looked like those of a nineteenth-century English twin-masted brig. The frames were double, and its ports were those of a merchant ship. Its length was about 90 feet, and the hold was about 16 feet deep. It also had a hole cut in its side.

To place the wreck of the *Isabella* on the National Register of Historic Places, which would protect it, SCRU had to explain why it was particularly significant. The archaeologists concluded that the *Isabella* was the only known vessel of this type ever located in the United States. It also contained the only "encapsuled" (completely contained) cargo from the Hudson's Bay Company ever found. This would give archaeologists the first glimpse into how the Hudson's Bay Company supplied and provided for its outposts. From the material on board, archaeologists can then move backward to expand and

Artist's rendering of the sunken *Isabella*

enrich the written historical records.

Because there has only been enough money to document the site, the *Isabella* continues to lie on the Columbia River bottom, holding onto its secrets and its booty for future generations to explore.

LOATHSOME PIRATES

Without the help of these fierce, deadly pirate captains, many of the wrecks lying on the ocean's floor would never have survived to tell their tales of the past to today's archaeologists. It's a costly debt we owe to these ruthless sea wolves.

The Brothers Barbarossa (Redbeard) - These two Barbary pirates raided the African coast during the sixteenth century, buying off the sultan of Tunisia for a sheltered hideaway to stow their ill-gotten gain.

Captain William Kidd - Probably the most famous pirate of all and captain of the *Adventure Galley*. Kidd's exploits were the inspiration for Robert Lewis Stevenson's book, *Treasure Island*. Kidd also plied his trade along the Hudson River and New York City. It was here he was captured by the governor of New York and returned to England, where he was hanged for piracy.

Sir Henry Morgan - A Welsh buccaneer (so called after *buccaning*, a method used by Indians to sun-dry meat) who plundered the West Indies trade ships and was best known for his sacking of the city of Panama.

Henry Jennings - Another Welshman who raided the Spanish Plate fleet, which brought supplies from Spain to the New World and returned to Spain with the spoils collected from the colonies. A hurricane dashed the fleet on the tip of Florida, and Jennings stormed in behind to loot the entire treasure.

Jean Lafitte - A French pirate, Lafitte ran his operation from a small island 50 miles from New Orleans. In 1814, when the British asked him to help them attack New Orleans, Lafitte informed the Americans of the pending battle and fought with the Americans to defeat the British. Because of his help, his pirating crimes were pardoned by President James Madison.

Edward Teach a.k.a. Thatch or Blackbeard - One of the meanest pirates to sail the seven seas, Blackbeard prospered along the Carolina and Florida coasts in the early 1700s. His name came from his long braided beard, which made him look even more ferocious—all the better to terrify his captives.

Calico Jack Rackman, Anne Bonny, and Mary Read - Rackman, a pirate captain in the Caribbean, was called Calico Jack because of the striped pants he wore. He was also the only pirate captain to have two women as crew members - Anne Bonny and Mary Read. Bonny and Read are the only known women pirates.

THE BARK Frances

THE BARK *FRANCES*

Loaded with tin and sugar that had been picked up in Singapore, the bark *Frances* had set sail from Calcutta, India, in August 1872, heading toward Boston harbor. It sailed around the Cape of Good Hope and made the crossing of the Atlantic Ocean with the blessing of a steady wind. From the Bahamian islands, the *Frances* headed north.

Three days after Christmas in 1872, a wintery storm raged along the New England seaboard, pummeling the Cape Cod coast. Just off Head-of-the-Meadow Beach was the *Frances*, a three-masted, square-sailed, iron-hulled ship built in Germany. A blasting, persistent northeaster smacked the vessel, and there was snow everywhere. 'Twas not a fit night for sailor or beast. The *Frances*'s captain, Kortling, lay ill in his cabin, ravaged by a disease he had picked up in Calcutta.

The storm easily tossed the *Frances* about as she tried to maneuver around the cape. Finally, it ran her aground 200 feet from the beach, where her iron hull quickly sank into the sandy bottom.

A rescue boat was dispatched from the shore, as the local citizens rushed to aid the *Frances*. The ailing captain was lowered

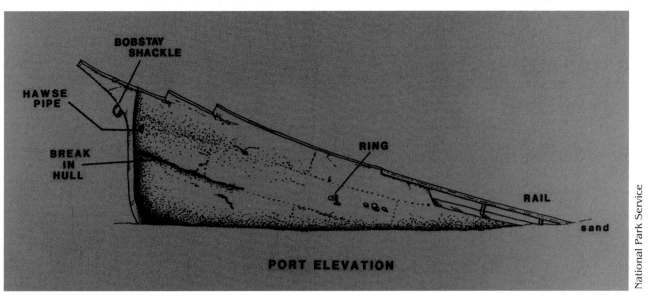

BOBSTAY SHACKLE

HAWSE PIPE

BREAK IN HULL

RING

RAIL

sand

PORT ELEVATION

National Park Service

into the lurching rescue boat. The waves threatened to smash it against the iron hull of the crippled bark. Four days later, Captain Kortling died from a combination of disease and exposure. All that was salvaged from the ship were a few stores and "200 baskets of sugar." All else was lost, as the ship eventually sank beneath the breakers.

Since it was lying in shallow water, the location of the *Frances* was never lost from public record. During calm seas, in fact, the remains of the hull often stuck out of the 15-foot-deep water.

As an underwater archaeological site, the *Frances* is an amazing time capsule of a late-nineteenth-century trading vessel. The square-sailed ship's iron hull is still intact, and its cargo of tin ingots is largely undisturbed. Largely, because some modern day scoundrels were arrested when they tried to remove some of the ingots. Nonetheless, this is an extraordinary example of a bark that sailed during the glory days of merchant sailing ships.

Although the *Frances* is in fairly shallow water, the site is still considered to be very dangerous. Archaeologists had to contend with the pounding surf and the water's low visibility. These two obstacles make diving extremely risky. If a diver dives at the wrong time or on the wrong day, he can easily end up, as Dan Lenihan, principal investigator for the SCRU, described it, "being run through a sieve" because of the ship's fractured metal hull.

Because of these treacherous waters, the *Frances* has never been excavated. One salvage company proposed to haul the ship's cargo out after using ultrasonic technology to document the strength of the ship's structure. By bouncing high-pitched sound waves off the vessel, they were able to determine if the ship would fall apart during excavation. But the SCRU's policy of preserving wrecks as important archaeological sites prevailed, and the salvage company's plan was turned down. The history contained within the *Frances* remains where it will be safe, beneath the waves.

National Park Service

Videotaping the *Frances* wreckage

THE BRIG LEONORA

THE ROGUE BULLY HAYES AND THE SINKING OF THE *LEONORA*

Bully Hayes sailed the seas of the South Pacific pillaging, plundering, scheming, and for all his wicked ways, he always escaped the law.

On April 1, 1870, Hayes pulled the ultimate April Fool's joke on those who had caught him stealing men and women from an island near Samoa. He persuaded the American Consul to allow him to inspect some navigating equipment aboard a ship captained by a friend of his. That night, Bully and his partner, Ben Pease, quietly slipped away from the authorities aboard Pease's ship, the *Pioneer*.

These two rogues slaved and traded together until Pease was arrested and jailed in Manila. Hayes took over the *Pioneer*. After stripping the boat of many of its trimmings and tearing its sails, Hayes brought the *Pioneer* into Shanghai, where the company that owned the ship resided. The company was in a dreadful state itself and decided to sell the ailing craft to Hayes for less than $800. They also paid the *Pioneer's* crew and completely refitted

the ship. They then directed Hayes to close out Ben Pease's trading stations throughout the South Pacific. Hayes did so, but instead of returning the money to the company, he kept it for himself. He repainted the *Pioneer* white and renamed her the *Leonora*.

For the next two years, Hayes operated a coconut and coconut oil trading business between the South Sea islands and San Francisco. During this time, there is no record of Hayes running afoul of the law.

On March 12, 1874, Hayes arrived at Kosrae, the easternmost island in the Caroline island chain. He found that the islands' 400 inhabitants were being terrorized by a group from some neighboring islands under the direction of five white men. With just the slightest of threats to open fire on their homes and completely destroy them, Hayes convinced the marauders to accompany him to an island nearby. He promised to set them up in the coconut processing business. Hayes convinced them this offered better opportunities than terrorizing Kosraeans.

On March 15, they all boarded the *Leonora* and headed around Kosrae to Utwe Harbor to gather pigs and yams for the trip. But just as they were getting ready to leave, a fierce storm started brewing. Hayes knew that if the *Leonora* remained anchored in the harbor, she'd be swamped. He gave orders to sail to open sea immediately. Unfortunately, his way was blocked by two whaling ships that didn't want to tempt the high surf that was battering them. Hayes was forced to ride out the storm in the harbor.

Clouds as black as pitch opened up on them, and high seas burst across the ship. The *Leonora* spun around on its anchor as it was tossed about. Finally, Hayes gave the order to abandon ship. It was recorded that Hayes, another man, and seven native women packed guns and ammunition, Hayes's time-keeping instruments and charts, and about 6,000 silver dollars onto one of the small boats on board. The women then managed, against all odds, to make it safely to land.

The furious storm mercilessly tossed the *Leonora*. It loosened two of her cannons. They crashed across the ship and rammed against the cannons on the other side, plowing them right through the bulwarks that held them in place. The *Leonora* was dashed onto a reef, sending the rudder through the deck. Then a huge wave swept Hayes and two remaining women over the stern of the ship. They were able to finally make it to shore. The *Leonora* was lost, its remaining goods plundered by the Kosraeans before she slipped beneath the waters of the harbor.

The wreck of the *Leonora*

A little over one hundred years later, in February 1981, the Submerged Cultural Resources Unit was called to Utwe Harbor to perform the archaeological field study on what was thought to be the wreck of the *Leonora*. During their first dive, after about 40 minutes, archaeologists found the wreck lying about 25 to 30 feet beneath the surface, against a coral reef. They took photographs and explored the general area of the site. The next day, three divers began the mapping procedures. Each visible feature of the wreck site was examined, measured, and photographed. Nothing on the site was disturbed. A videotape was also made. SCRU's Lenihan feels videotaping has become the most important scientific instrument underwater archaeologists now have. It allows them to study at length both the cultural features and the natural formations on the wreck site.

Archaeologists preparing to document the *Leonora* site

It was fairly certain after the preliminary work that these were in fact the remains of the *Leonora*. Most of the ship was buried in the silty bottom of the harbor, but remnants of a metal-covered box, probably one of the water tanks that had been noted on the ship's manifest when Hayes took command of the *Leonora*, were visible. In all, nine major features were discovered, including some of the 50 tons of stone used for the ship's ballast. They also found parts of the ship's hull and a number of the structural elements.

Even though most of the site was covered with silt and coral, the *Leonora*'s storm-shattered remains were in excellent shape, with very little human disturbance. But because of limited resources, the SCRU decided to leave the *Leonora* and its site undisturbed. Excavation is a very expensive and delicate process, and unless enough money is available to do the job properly, SCRU's Lenihan believes "the right place for it is the place it's in." The silt of Utwe Harbor has protected Bully Hayes's pride and joy for one hundred years, and it will continue to do so. In the meantime, the Kosraeans living in Utwe Harbor are actively protecting the site.

Eventually, the SCRU plans to unlock the treasure chest of history and science on board the *Leonora*. The information they hope to gather will add tremendously to our knowledge of life and navigation on the wild South Seas. It will also provide us with a more accurate picture of one of the most famous rogues of the high seas, Bully Hayes.

In the meantime, plans are being considered to turn this site into a protected underwater trail. As a model, the SCRU would use its *Windjammer* site that is at the heart of the Fort Jefferson underwater trail in Florida.

One of the *Leonora*'s water tanks

MIDSHIPS WRECKAGE

STARBOARD HULL SIDE

STEAM
MACHINERY

HULL BOTTOM

CENTERLINE
KEELSON

TOPSAIL YARD

BILGE
KEELSONS

LOWER YARD

FOREMAST

LOWER PART
OF FOREMAST

FOREMAST
CHAINPLATES

LADDER

HATCH COAMING

PORT HULL SIDE

DECK
STANCHIONS

BILGE
CEILING

BILGE KEELSON

MACHINERY
(BELOW)

FRESH
WATER TANK

CAPSTAN

CENTERLINE KEELSON

MIDSHIPS WRECKAGE

CHAINPLATES

LOWER YARD

BOW WRECKAGE

STARBOARD HULL SIDE

MAIN CHAINPLATES

MAIN MAST

LOWER YARD

BOWSPRIT

TOPSAIL YARD

ANCHOR

FEET
0   10   20   30   40   50

DATA FOR THIS DRAWING OBTAINED THROUGH
PROJECT SEAMARK, A COOPERATIVE EFFORT OF
NATIONAL PARK SERVICE AND THE UNITED STATES NAVY
(MOBILE DIVING AND SALVAGE UNIT TWO, DET. 506).

WINDJAMMER SITE
FORT JEFFERSON NATIONAL MONUMENT
DRY TORTUGAS, FLORIDA

DRAWN BY LARRY NORDBY

THE NATIONAL PARK SERVICE
SUBMERGED CULTURAL RESOURCES UNIT

WINDJAMMER SITE—FORT JEFFERSON TRAIL

Located on Loggerhead Reef just off Loggerhead Key, Florida, this underwater national park site has a remarkable underwater trail, complete with underwater guide and map (pictured above) of a 300-foot wrecked sailing ship that went down in the early 1900s.

33

USS ARIZONA

THE USS *ARIZONA*

Out of the rising sun they appeared, 360 Japanese war planes, and the surprise attack on Pearl Harbor, on the Hawaiian island of Oahu, was under way. In less than an hour on December 7, 1941, fourteen ships were sunk, including the battleship USS *Arizona*, which went down with 1,177 sailors on board. The surprise attack on Pearl Harbor brought the United States into World War II.

In 1983, forty-two years after the *Arizona*'s sinking, the Submerged Cultural Resources Unit was called in to map and photodocument the wreck. A national memorial shrine had been built on top of the remains, but no one knew the actual condition of the *Arizona*. What was the state of the hull? Was the battleship about to fall apart? Where was the leaking oil coming from? Were there any weapons or live ammunition still on board? A great deal of recent history was lying on the bottom of Pearl Harbor. What could it tell us about what actually happened on that tragic day?

SCRU's documentation would eventually become a tool for those who run the memorial to educate the public. It would also give archaeologists information about how humans acted and reacted during a modern surprise attack. To accomplish this, the SCRU carefully documented everything they found, including the debris that had been dropped from the memorial above and was now lying on deck. It was a formidable task.

They prepared themselves for a risky operation. Because of the underwater explosions that had rocked the area, the escaping oil, and the unexploded ammunition that they assumed was still on board, the *Arizona* site had a reputation for being very dangerous. But it proved to be less dangerous than was originally thought.

Measuring the USS *Arizona* site

National Park Service photo by Larry Murphy

The SCRU began its ten-day site assessment and immediately discovered there were many things we didn't know about the *Arizona*. The navy had thought that all the big guns on the ship had been salvaged. On SCRU's very first dive, they found the No. 1 turret with its 14-inch guns still intact. Included in this find, located right under the memorial, in fact, were an incredible number of live 5-inch shells. These were immediately removed.

The diving conditions were far from ideal. Visibility in the water is only 5 to 7 feet, and the *Arizona* is located at a depth of about 40 feet. From the preliminary information obtained, the SCRU was able to set up the procedures for the extensive mapping that would be conducted the following year.

For four weeks in 1984, the SCRU dodged tourist boats in the area as they took on the massive task of completely mapping the

USS *Arizona* Memorial

No. 1 turret, 14-inch gun

Artist's rendering of the bombing damage to the USS *Arizona*, with memorial shown at top right

608-foot-long ship. Compare the size of the *Arizona* with the 90-foot-long *Isabella*, and you can imagine how much more work there was to do. Over a half mile of nylon string was used, and thousands of measurements were taken.

Because the SCRU was using a large number of people who were experienced divers but who did not have scientific training, their methods for recording their findings were very low tech. For the most part, they used string and numbered clothespins as measurement devices. The exceptional results of their efforts show that low tech was the right tech.

The SCRU decided not to enter the *Arizona*. The added risk of diving in places where a roof exists is too great. Divers can become completely disoriented and might spend an hour trying in their panic to get out of a closet-sized room. Enough lives had already been lost on the *Arizona*.

At one point, the archaeologists ran into a problem. Their string-line measurements showed that two features on the *Arizona* were wider apart than on the original construction plans. Using an electronic measuring device, called an infrared theodolite, they confirmed that their underwater string measurements were correct. They were then able to determine that the ship had expanded at the explosion point, just like a tin can that becomes overpressurized.

You might think that everything would already be known about the life and times of a ship that had gone down during a battle only forty years before. But the remains of the *Arizona*, together with those of the other sunken vessels in Pearl Harbor, offered a physical account of World War II that could never be found in books or on film.

Mapping the wreckage

Top and bottom: National Park Service photos by Larry Murphy

LESSONS LEARNED

We have learned a great deal about how to preserve our sub-merged cultural resources from the SCRU documentation of the *Arizona*. Before this work began, there were no guide-lines for preservation. Afterward, a plan was drawn up to properly manage the site, to protect it for ages to come. The plan allowed scientists to determine such things as how fast the ship was deteriorating, ways of mapping any growths on the ship, and what long-term steps should be taken to preserve the site.

The science of underwater archaeology is still relative-ly young: it has emerged in the past 30 years with the development of scuba gear. From each experience, the SCRU learns more about the process, the questions they should ask, and how to respect and protect the historical remains they encounter. We have all become very concerned about protecting our land-based environment and its varied and many archaeological treasures. Now we are beginning to think of better ways to protect our underwater environment and its treasures, too.

Checking for structural deterioration

ocumenting a wreck off the Apostle Islands

The Submerged Cultural Resource Unit's main job is to manage the historic treasures lying on the river bottoms, lakebeds, and seafloors of the world. That means the SCRU must know where these sunken wrecks are, what they are, how important they are, and how the SCRU can best serve the future in caring for these sites.

The important thing to remember is that many of these shipwrecks occurred over one hundred years ago. There is no hurry to dig them up. There comes a point in a shipwreck's deterioration when there is little danger that future storms will cause further damage. So the greatest threat to these sites is generally from humans. Sometimes the best management decision is to simply leave them alone.

Cultural resource management is a way of appreciating the relics of the past as important and valuable parts of our environment. It is preserving and protecting them, too, just as we would the natural part of our environment. Cultural resource management allows us to look at that past as a part of our national heritage, a heritage that we need to care for and understand.

The National Park Service makes no distinction between those treasures that are on land—like Yellowstone National Park, the Grand Canyon, Bandelier, and Mt. Rushmore—and those that are underwater—like Fort Jefferson, Isle Royale, or the USS *Arizona*. In some cases, those national treasures that are underwater are more valuable links to the past because they have been less abused and spoiled by "civilization."

There are laws that protect them. The shipwrecks on National Park Service land are sheltered by the laws that established the National Park Service. All other wrecks are protected by the Abandoned Shipwreck Act of 1987. This act states that these wrecks are part of the national history, and those who tamper with them are breaking the law. The modern scalawags who were recently arrested on the *Frances* were in violation of the Abandoned Shipwreck Act. After many abuses, we are finally learning to protect these valuable sunken treasures of our past. ❧

National Park Service

**Members of the
SCRU staff**

THE SPOILERS—SALVAGERS AND TREASURE HUNTERS

ike scavengers of the sea, they loot and sack and spoil the underwater environment. They are the treasure hunters and the salvagers. Not interested in the science and history to be carefully uncovered, they ruin these underwater sites for the ages. They know there's a buck to be made from the relics and treasures of the past. So they harvest the buried antiquities (which truly belong to everyone) and sell them. In most cases, these shipwreck grave robbers are operating within the law. That doesn't mean that what they are doing is responsible or that their methods of harvesting are not destructive.

If these people were to try what they are doing on land, say, by going into Carlsbad Caverns and trying to take out some stalactites for someone's living room, they would be thrown in jail. To survey and excavate a sunken ship properly is very expensive. It takes careful planning and a great deal of time and experience. Treasure hunters go in fast and dirty, often taking the last remaining bits of archaeological significance. In Florida, where most of the remaining Spanish shipwrecks have been looted, we have lost a part of our heritage we will never be able to recover. Like the pirates who plundered the tops of the seas, these salvagers have raided the bottom.

CRU Bikini shipwreck study

THE UNDERWATER NATIONAL PARKS

There are sixty-one national parks with submerged cultural resources. Twenty-six of them contain shipwrecks. If you and your family are interested in visiting these parks (to dive you must be certified), you should check ahead with the park to make sure the underwater sites are accessible. Some of these sites can be explored with mask, snorkel, and fins.

The sites are rated: ✌ = good diving, 👆 = advanced diving skills are required or the diving is mediocre, and ♦ = no diving allowed

WESTERN REGION
Channel Islands National Park, California ✌
Golden Gate National Recreation Area, California 👆
Point Reyes National Seashore, California 👆
War in the Pacific National Historical Park, Guam ✌
USS *Arizona* Memorial, Hawaii ♦

SOUTHEAST REGION
Biscayne National Monument, Florida ✌
Fort Jefferson National Monument, Florida ✌
Gulf Islands National Seashore, Florida ✌
Virgin Islands National Park, Virgin Islands ✌
Buck Island Reef National Monument, Virgin Islands ✌
Cape Hatteras National Seashore, North Carolina 👆
Cape Lookout National Seashore, North Carolina 👆

SOUTHWEST REGION
Padre Island National Seashore, Texas 👆

MIDWEST REGION
Indiana Dunes National Lakeshore, Indiana 👆
Isle Royale National Park, Michigan ✌
Pictured Rocks National Lakeshore, Michigan ✌
Sleeping Bear Dunes National Lakeshore, Michigan ✌
Apostle Islands National Lakeshore, Wisconsin ✌

ROCKY MOUNTAIN REGION
Glen Canyon National Recreation Area, Arizona ✌

National Park Service photo by Ann Belleman

NORTH ATLANTIC REGION

Cape Cod National Seashore, Massachusetts ✌
Fire Island National Seashore, New York ☝
Gateway National Recreation Area, New Jersey ☝

MID-ATLANTIC REGION

Assateague Island National Seashore, Maryland ☝

NORTHWEST REGION

Fort Vancouver National Historic Site, Washington ☝
San Juan Island National Historical Park, Washington ☝

The bow of the Windjammer wreck, Loggerhead Key

National Park Service

National Park Service

AFTERWORD

Sailing the oceans blue has never been without its risks. The sea is a fickle friend at best—calm and obliging one minute, raging and cater-wauling the next. She has been the final resting spot for many a sailor and many a fine ship. She holds these treasures in safekeeping, returning their precious contents to those who find it first. To some, this sunken booty is money in the pocket. To others, scientists and historians, these remains are pure, unpolluted pictures of the past, a part of our heritage, belonging to everyone. If the lure of seafaring adventure is in your bones, remember this:

Spoil, and the treasures are lost forever.
Preserve, and we all share in the wealth.

Video documentation of a shipwreck

National Park Service

GLOSSARIZED INDEX

Abandoned Shipwreck Act of 1987 38
Africa 9
Air molecules 12
Anchor 8
Apple-cheeked - an apple-shaped, puffy bow, 25-26
Aquanauts 11
Archaeologist - a person who studies past human life, 2,4,7,8,9,18,24,25,26,29,31,34, 36
Archaeology 1,13
Archaios - ancient things, 1
Artifacts - objects crafted by humans, 2
Astronauts 11
Adventure Galley - Captain Kidd's ship, 27
Bahamian Islands 28
Ballast - the heavy weights stored in the bottom of a ship to keep it steady, 3,8,9
Bandelier National Monument 38
Bark - a three-masted ship, 28-29
Battle frigate - a square-rigged warship, 8
Bends - also called decompression sickness, this condition occurs when a diver rises to the surface from great depths too quickly, 15
Bilge - the very bottom of a boat, where the ballast is stored, 3,8,9,25
Bluebeard 8,18
Bonny, Anne 27
Brig, twin-masted 22, 25,26
Brothers Barbarossa 27
Buccaneer - another name for a pirate, refers to an Indian approach to drying meat that was eaten by these pirates, 27
Bulwarks - the holes on the sides of ships through which cannons are fired, 8,31
Buoyancy compensators 16
Buoyant - able to float, 16
Calcutta 28
Camera 2
Cannons 8, 31
Cape Horn 22
Cape Cod 28
Cape of Good Hope 28
Cargo 2,3,6,7,24,25,29
Carlsbad Caverns 39
Carolina Islands 30
Clipper - tall and very fast sailing ship, 4
Clothespins 18,36
Coffers - a chest used to store valuables, 6
Columbia bar 25
Columbia River 22,24,25
Columbia River Maritime Museum 24
Compressed air - air that has been compacted and stored in tanks for breathing underwater, 13
Computers 18
Construction 2,3,25
Cook boxes 8
Cousteau, Jacques - well known for his contributions to our knowledge of the oceans and one of the developers of scuba gear, 13
Cultural resource management - a way of appreciating and protecting the resources of the past, 38
Currents 26
Decompression - releasing the body from pressure, 15
Decompression sickness - also called the "bends," 15
Decompression tables - tables that detail how long a diver must decompress after a dive, 15
Deep-sea divers 11
Diving knife 16
Diving watch 16

Dry suits 11,16,26
Eustachian tube - the tube that leads from the throat to the middle ear, 13
Fins 11,13
Forged - formed by heating and hammering, 4
Fort Jefferson Underwater Trail 32,33,38
Founder - to sink, 8
Frances 28,29,38
Gagnan, Emil - one of the developers of scuba gear, 13
Galleon - a Spanish sailing vessel, 3
Gauges - measuring devices, 14,16
Gloves 16
Gold Rush 4
Grand Canyon 38
Hallucinate - to see things that aren't really there, 15
Hayes, Bully 30,32
Head-of-the-Meadow beach - final resting place for the bark *Frances*, 28
Hold - the place on a ship where cargo is stored, 6,7
Hoods 16
Hudson's Bay Company 22,24,26
Hudson River 27
Hull - the outside base of a ship, 3,32,34
Infrared theodolite - a high-tech measuring device, 36
Innovation - a new approach, 5
Iron hull 28-29
Isabella 22,23,25,26,36
Isle Royale 38
Jennings, Henry 27
Jolly Roger - a pirate's skull and crossbones flag, 8
Kidd, Captain William 27
Kortling, Captain 28-29
Kosrae 30, 31,32
Lafitte, Jean 27
Laser beams 18, 20
Laser imaging process - using lasers to map an object, 20
Lead weights 16
Lenihan, Dan 29,31,32
Leonora 30,31,32
Loggerhead Key 33
Loggerhead Reef 33
Logos - to know all about, 1
Lungs 13
Madison, James 27
Mainsail - the primary sail on the mainmast, 22
Manifest - the list of cargo on a ship, 7
Manila 30
Mapping procedures 31
Mask 11, 13
Mast 22,28
Masthead - the top of the mast, 2
Measuring tapes 18
Merchant ship 25,26
Midden - trash piles, 9
Middle ear 13
Morgan, Sir Henry 27
Mouthpiece 14
Mt. Rushmore 38
National Park Service 22,38
National Register of Historic Places 26
Nitrogen 15
Nitrogen absorption - the accumulation of nitrogen in the body that takes place when diving at a depth greater than 30 feet, 15,19
Oahu, Hawaii 34
Pacific Ocean 25
Pearl Harbor 34,36
Pease, Ben 30

Pioneer 30
Port side - the left side of a ship, 8
Protractor - a device for drawing angles, 18
Rackman, Calico Jack 27
Read, Mary 27
Regulator - the mechanism that adjusts the flow of compressed air from an air tank so a diver can safely breathe it, 13,14
Relic - an object that has survived a long time, 1
Remote operated vehicle (ROV) 20
Rigging - the lines that move sails and masts, 2,8
Robots 20
Ryan, Captain William 22
Samoa 30
Sand Island 25,26
Santa Maria de la Rosa - a ship of the Spanish Armada, 8
Scavengers and salvagers 39
Schnorchel 11
SCUBA - self-contained underwater breathing apparatus, 13
Shanghai 30
SHARPS (sonic highly accurate range position system) 20
Singapore 28
Slack tides - those tides that come between high and low tide, 25
Snorkel - a manual breathing device, 11,13
South Seas 9
Spanish Armada 8
Spanish plate fleet - a fleet of Spanish vessels that carried precious metals back to Spain from the New World, 27
Square-sailed 28-29
Steam power 5
Stevenson, Robert Lewis 27
Stores 2, 7,25
String 18, 36
Submarines 11
Submerged Cultural Resource Unit (SCRU) 22,24,29,32,34,36,38,40
Submersible—a small underwater vehicle for working in deep and frigid waters, 20
Swivel guns 8
Tanks 13
Teach, Edward (a.k.a. Thatch or Blackbeard) 27
Titanic 5
Trim - make ready for sailing, 2, 8
Ultrasonic technology 29
Underwater compass 16
USS Arizona 34,36
Utwe Harbor 31,32
Valve - a device that opens and closes the flow of air to a diver's regulator, 13,14
Vessels 3
Video camera 2, 20
Warship 25
Water molecules 12
Water pressure 14,15
Weapons 2, 8, 34
Wet suits 16, 26
William & Ann 22
Windjammer 32,33
Yarn - a tall tale, 1
Yellowstone National Park 38